JESUS WOMEN

Irene Sayer

Dedication

This book is dedicated to
Women's Network of the Methodist Church
East Anglia District

Jesus Women

Jesus included women among his friends which was unusual for a man of his day. For three years some were part of his travelling team. Did they shop and cook for Jesus and his disciples? Wash their clothes, look after and care about them?

Some of their names we know. A few were relatives. One was a woman with a past, while others were well respected for their faith and hospitality. Some we glimpse briefly, coming in and out of Jesus' life. A few stayed the course, even up to his death.

All had this in common: they were Jesus Women. He touched their lives.

As we look together, perhaps we will identify with some of them.

My aim is that we, though we are all very different, will be inspired to love Jesus more and more. To give what we have to offer to be used by God's Spirit. To become today's Jesus Women.

Irene Sayer
August 2003

Contents

The PUSHY Woman
Matthew 9:18-22

On the only occasion we read about her, this woman pushed her way in. Jesus was her last chance. For 12 years, 4,380 days, blood had flowed from her body. Having spent every penny she had on doctors, she prayed daily for deliverance. This constant show of blood had depleted her strength, worn her out, putting her on the fringe of society with no husband to protect her. A menstruating woman was considered unclean and excluded from worship, as was anyone she touched. When hope had faded of a 'normal' life, she heard about Jesus. Well, let's face it, everyone in her area had heard about Jesus! People reported his wonderful words, and miraculous healings. What had interested her most was his attitude to women. He was unique, in that he included them in his immediate group. If she could get close enough to talk to him and tell him about her plight, surely he would be the one man who would listen, not because she paid him to, like the physicians, but because he cared.

She went in search of him. So had everyone else! A crowd always surrounded him. She eventually saw him deep in conversation with a wealthy man. She saw him turn round and stride off purposefully. She was going to miss him! She pushed through the crowd. Yes, pushed through. The woman who had always held back, avoiding others for fear of contaminating them as the Law suggested.

The last few steps were a nightmare. As he was moving away from her, she threw herself forward and touched the hem of his garment. He stopped. 'Who touched me?' he said. People surrounded him, pressing in on every side. 'Someone touched me, I felt the power go out of me.'

He looked down, straight into her face. There was an electric moment of recognition. In that brief second, she looked on the face of God. Even before he spoke the words, she knew she was healed. She told him the whole story. All the hurt, pain, and rejection. As their eyes locked she felt she was the most important person in his life at that moment, so undivided was his attention. 'Daughter, go in peace, your faith has healed you. Be free from your suffering,' he said.

And she was.

Being pushy paid off for her that day.

Some people think it unbecoming in a woman to be pushy. It depends on the circumstances, I'd say.

There are times when we need to be philosophical about our lives, accepting our lot. Not always. I guess the trick must be to know the difference!

I have a lot in common with this particular pushy woman, strangely enough for similar reasons.

She obviously could not conceive. She had no hope of children, which was very sad in a society where women had little status until they had sons.

Many women will know the disappointment that can come with every monthly period. Realising early in our marriage that the longed-for family of our own was just a dream, I began visiting the fertility clinic, and I prayed. How I prayed! What a blessing that God has a generous heart. I took up so much of his time in those days! So many women in the Bible would have known exactly how I felt. An Old Testament word was 'desolate'. It was impossible to believe that this was God's will for me. Had he not said in Psalm 113: 'He gives the barren woman a home, making her the joyous mother of children'?

I claimed that promise for myself, hanging on like a terrier! In 1970 we became foster-parents with Norfolk Social Services Department.

The first two children placed with us were twins, nine and a half year old girls. They had had a very unstable childhood and were in a children's home on the north Norfolk coast. We lived in a farmhouse with lots of room and animals. The girls had a few problems, but considering that they had to get used to new people, a new home, strange surroundings and a different school, they both did remarkably well. We had our ups and downs and several mutinies, but on the whole we all enjoyed our new life together. With their lovely singing voices and willingness to take part in services, as preachers we felt blessed. They became favourites around the Diss Circuit. They were bright, attractive and were doing well at the local school.

A year later, on 23rd August 1971, their social worker came to tell us that their parents were asking for them back. During their six years in a children's home and in the year they lived with us, their parents had visited them once. A year is time enough to love someone. When we accepted, after strenuous effort, that we could not change the decision, we very reluctantly let them go.

On surely the most unhappy of my husband Roy's birthdays, we took Jan and Sue, with their acquired paraphernalia, to Birmingham and handed them over to their parents. Returned to our empty home, the void was unfillable. Over the years all pain recedes, but writing this now, 30 years on, I discover the scars have not quite healed.

I dropped into the routine of cooking for two, not four, the washing and ironing halved. The peace and quiet, which formerly in noisy moments I had longed for, was deafening.

I stabbed my finger at the text from Psalm 113. Where was the 'joyous mother of children'? I spent a fair bit of time shaking my fist in God's face, and then apologising! Still he loved me, sending the most amazing comfort, though it took me years to realise it.

Immediately after this, I was involved in an Evangelical Mission. Talk about putting on a brave face! I remember two little lads from the children's meetings who gave their lives to Jesus. God's strength was in my weakness.

Returning a few weeks later from helping my friend with her daughter's party, our social worker was waiting for me. On hearing that I had been helping a group with special needs, he asked, 'Are you interested in disabled children?' What a loaded question! Three babies with Down's syndrome, recently born in the area, had been rejected at birth. When we went to be introduced to one of them, both Roy and I remember experiencing a feeling of inevitability. At nearly three months old Claire weighed 8lbs 13oz. Learning to feed and care for her was a terrifying experience! But gradually my confidence increased and a few weeks later we brought her home. We discovered Claire had been born on 23rd August. The very day the social worker had told us the twins were going. Divine coincidence? The significance of the shared date brought me comfort.

It was a strange time. Suddenly a mum, but no cards of congratulations, no little knitted cardigans. When I went shopping with the pram, people would walk over and look in. Mostly there was silence as they realised that Claire was disabled. I guess they didn't know what to say. I always said it for them. 'She doing really well, for a baby with Down's syndrome', letting them know it was OK to mention it!

Still feeling cheated, I suffered a bout of depression. I had asked my Father for bread and he had given me a stone. I had all the limitations of motherhood but few of the rewards.

Prior to having Claire we had children to stay from the inner cities, on The Country Holiday Scheme. Loving the experience, we regretted that they wouldn't place children with us now because we had a disabled child. The Adoption Societies we applied to felt the same. We were a 'disabled family'. Even the Social Services Department hesitated about placing another child with us. We did have a boy suffering from micro-cephalous, who stayed for three months, and a few 'emergency' children.

It would be hard to convey the pain I was feeling at this time. We loved Claire and wanted her to be the best she could be. But wrongly or rightly it wasn't enough. How I bombarded God! Talk about a pushy woman!

When Claire was four and a half, her Social Worker rang: 'Now don't go overboard, Irene, we've had a baby brought into the office. Would you be prepared to have her for a few days?'

That was 26 years ago.

We adopted Claire and Lisa. The promise of Psalm 113 had been fulfilled.

For many years, I felt I had second-best. Looking back I realise that what appeared to be second-best for me was indeed first-best from God.

During that painful process, my 'religion' somehow changed into a 'relationship' with God.

Footnote: After 14 years of silence the twins contacted us.

A further footnote: At the time of writing there are almost 59,000 children 'in care' and of these 5,000 up for adoption.

The AMBITIOUS Woman
Matthew 20:20-28

Salome,* married to Zebedee, had two sons. They had a family fishing business. James and John, like their cousins Simon and Andrew, were fishermen. Their mum was very proud of them. Who wouldn't be? They were fine young men, hardworking and intelligent, fit and strong. Good boys, happy to work with their father. But one day Zebedee came home to tell her that the boys had gone. Dragged in the nets, unloaded and left.

Imagine the household that evening. The air was blue! Salome blamed Zebedee for not being ambitious enough. He should have paid them more, given the boys a freer hand. She blamed herself for not seeing it coming. Why would they want to leave home? Didn't she provide them with everything they needed? Wasn't she always looking out for them? Hadn't she lined up a couple of lovely girls for them to marry? She could almost see her grandchildren now.

Where had they gone? Had someone offered them a better deal?

No, said Zebedee wearily, they've gone with Jesus.

Gone with Jesus? What did he mean, gone with Jesus? Where? Why? What for? Which Jesus? Our Jesus? Mary's boy? Weren't they John the Baptist's disciples last week?

Did Zebedee have to screw up his courage to tell her that their nephews, Simon and Andrew from round the corner, had gone too?

Simon and Andrew? Had everyone gone mad?

Maybe Zebedee was glad to go fishing early the next morning, even if he was short-handed!

James and John were called the 'Sons of Thunder' – I wonder where that title came from?

6

Salome could not leave it there. The small group was easy enough to find, they never travelled far. Sitting on the edge of the crowd was hard. But as the days went by, her attitude changed. Her sons were changing too. They were happy and fulfilled as never before. Jesus had kept his promise that they would fish for men. She felt proud of them again, loving their assurance as they moved among the people and their excitement as they returned from their preaching trip. OK, they lived a bit rough. But they were so full of life and vitality.

She began to believe that Jesus was the promised Messiah.

As she watched her sons become close friends with Jesus, a new plan began to form in her mind.

Sure, she had heard Jesus talk about the first being last and the last being first, and recently on the way up to Jerusalem he had spoken about his death. But many times she heard him speak about his new kingdom. Kings had power; they needed the right people round them. Who better than her sons?

Gathering James and John, she went looking for Jesus.

She bowed. 'Please can I ask a favour?'

Jesus said, 'What is it you want?'

She answered, 'Grant that one of these two sons of mine may sit at your right and the other at your left in your kingdom.'

Not answering straight away, Jesus looked at the embarrassed faces of his two friends, and then back with such love at their ambitious mother. She was asking for the wrong things, but for the right reasons! How she loved these men! And so did he.

'You don't know what you are asking. Can you drink the cup I am going to drink?'

'We can,' they answered.

Jesus, choking back the emotion his foreknowledge gave him, said: 'You will indeed drink from my cup, but to sit at my right or left is not for me to grant. These places belong to those for whom they have been prepared by my father.'

She couldn't understand why the other disciples were upset. Didn't they realise how special her sons were?

A few days later, there was a carnival atmosphere as Jesus entered Jerusalem on a donkey. The crowd went wild, tearing branches from the olive trees, coming out of the city waving palm branches taken from the booths that lined the road. All this confirmed to Salome that Jesus was a man of destiny!

The dream turned sour. The following weeks were a blur of pain, disbelief and shame – yes, there, she had said it. Shame. How she burned with humiliation as she remembered her request of Jesus.

Salome was one of the women present at Jesus' death. As she looked at the three crosses, she registered the two villains crucified either side of Jesus. With dreadful realisation she knew, had they been arrested, it could have been her beloved James and John. One on his right hand and the other on his left.

Surely now it was over, they would come home. It may still be possible to pick up their old lives, the old dreams.

Looking back, she smiled to herself at her naivety. In Jerusalem, the risen Jesus had appeared to her frightened sons. The locked doors were thrown back. Indeed they did come home to Galilee and met Jesus there. She knew there was no stopping them now! Jesus still called them to leave everything, to stay in Jerusalem until they were filled with the power of God. Not the power she had dreamed of, had been ambitious for, but the power to be the very cornerstones of the Christian Church.

Little did she know that 2,000 years later, we would still be talking about her boys.

In the 1960s, women like me were encouraged to believe we could have everything. We had to have ambitions beyond the home and family. No longer were we appendages of our men. We could not only burn our bras, but we could be free. How strange that 'freedom' looks now. Of course, the reality of the man, woman, one boy, one girl family didn't always work, but neither, in fact, did this newfound 'freedom'.

Not all ambition is wrong. We would still be living in caves if someone hadn't had the ambition to change her lot. Women today have opportunities undreamed of by our grandmothers, and rightly so, too!

We understand Salome. We want our children to be the best they can be. But ambition should not be at the expense of our families. Some women try to live their lives through their children, pushing them to achieve the things they missed out on themselves.

It distresses me to see our very achievement-based education system putting such pressure on our young people.

A great lesson to learn in life is that we can't have it all, no matter what was promised us in the 60s. What we can have, and our birthright as Christian women, is what only a few Old Testament prophets and leaders experienced: the Spirit of the Living God poured out on all people, men, women and children. All the good things God offers us in Jesus Christ.

Above all we can have purpose, something that seems to be lacking in so many lives today. What we do with our ambition is more important. God has a plan for each of us. We are unique and special, and when we hand our lives over to him, he can make us the best that we can be.

Let every part of ourselves and our lives be a training for what he has in store for us. Nothing we live through is ever wasted.

I believe God's timing is perfect, no matter how slow he seems to be sometimes! It's worth waiting. We don't need to snatch at it all now.

Longing to travel, I remember sitting in Kew Gardens watching the planes soar overhead to their exotic destinations and praying, 'Let it soon be my turn, Lord.'

A week after my 50th birthday I flew to Africa for the first time. Our daughters were old enough and able enough to part with their Mum for a couple of weeks. Roy could cope, and since those days has even learned to cook! The timing was perfect and I have been able to use that experience to great effect in working for Fair Trade and development. The last 10 years have sped by, and I've travelled a lot.

Perhaps better than ambition, is to be driven.

Driven by love for God and the desire to be found doing his will.

* The author of Matthew's Gospel does not mention her name, but tradition calls the mother of John and James Salome.

The WANTON Woman
Luke 7:36-50

Imagine the scene. A sumptuous house with men reclining round the well-laden table. Everyone there at the request of a man called Simon, referred to as 'the Pharisee'. Jesus and his friends had been invited, mainly because Jesus was the latest celebrity in town. Perhaps Simon wanted to show how open-minded he was, perhaps he was just showing off. However, he made it clear that Jesus was not honoured and revered by his host. Simon hadn't even offered the usual formalities expected in a Jewish household. No water to wash the feet, no kiss of greeting.

Jesus was there under the critical gaze of Simon, who would have been happy to bring him down a peg or two.

Enter a prostitute. No beating about the bush. We are told she was a woman who sold sex for a living. Over the years art has been kind to this woman. Often portrayed wearing an extravagant blue gown, sometimes she is even wearing a halo! But make no mistake about it. She was a notorious 'sinner'.

As she came into the gathering there was a sharp intake of breath. Most of the people there knew who she was. Some of the men may even have availed themselves of her services. Perhaps they feared she would embarrass them. They needn't have worried. She wasn't looking at them. She only had eyes for Jesus. She knew what she was. She didn't need their approval or disapproval. She was sick of her soiled life and wanted a new start. Pouring oil and massaging men's bodies was not new to her. She was paid to do it all the time, among other things.

This one was on her. Jesus was always doing something for others: this woman was doing something for him. Something she was good at. But this time it was from choice. No bowl of perfumed water and flannel. Just the saltiness of her tears, which flowed unchecked from her reddened eyes. OK, she knew the rules; women never uncovered their long hair in public. But what did that matter? Her unbraided hair covered her swollen face as she leaned forward to wipe Jesus' feet. She couldn't speak. She didn't need to. All her regret, all her remorse was in her touch and her tears. With every kiss to his feet her heart was saying, 'Forgive me, help me, heal me, and make me like you.'

She sensed that Jesus was speaking, and his words brought joy to her heart. He told a story, a story so simple that anyone could understand. Jesus was directing it at Simon, but she knew it was for her.

'Two men owed money to a certain moneylender. One owed him 500 denarii, and the other 50. Neither of them had the money to pay him back, so he cancelled the debt of both. Now, which of them will love him more?'

'I suppose the one who had the bigger debt cancelled,' said Simon.

She hardly heard Jesus chastising Simon, and praising her, until he looked directly at her and said: 'Your sins are forgiven.'

That's what she longed to hear. His love flowed into her life, giving her the power to turn her back on her past and begin again.

Those of us who are fortunate enough to have been married to someone who loves and values us should never take this for granted, or ever be tempted to look down on another's lifestyle.

This was brought home to me 10 years ago when I went to Nairobi for the first time. The Traidcraft group I was with visited Maridadi Fabrics, one of their trading partners. The workshop was in a very sleazy part of town. Pumwami was a piece of land given by the then British Government, to house the prostitutes needed to service the British forces. Pumwami Slum, as it is now, is still home to many women selling sex. In 1999 the going price was 50 shillings (50p) for unprotected sex and 60 shillings (60p)if a condom was used.

Every one of the workers at Maridadi Fabrics was a former prostitute. Christians had initiated the workshop, designed to teach the women skills in screen printing and tailoring. They produced beautiful fabric and garments, which were sold through the Fair Trade Movement. Some local hotels purchased this African-designed material for curtains and tablecloths. The ladies also made school uniforms.

When I listened to the women and heard their stories, I was filled with admiration. In a male dominated country, where polygamous men can discard the mother of their children for no reason other than wanting a newer wife, these women left their villages and found their way to Nairobi. With children crying round their skirts for food and water, they had only their bodies to sell.

Through Maridadi Fabrics, all the women had moved out of the slum. All had educated their children, some even to university standard!

Judge them? Who, me? I was too full of admiration to judge them. I remember their dignity and pride.

This same Jesus, who offered forgiveness and a new start to the woman in the story, lives on in Christians today. That's one of the reasons I am so passionate about the opportunities offered by Fair Trade: working opportunities that give women dignity and choice.

Traidcraft, a Christian initiative, last year turned over more than £10 million. Yet in the same year we spent £67 billion in supermarkets! I wish more people would see for themselves what a difference it makes to invest in people. Strange that people can't understand why I get upset when I see non Fair Trade products in church kitchens!

Whether we have been forgiven much or little, we have all been included in the sacrifice of Jesus. God help us to love much.

More importantly, God help us to put our faith into action.

The PRACTICAL Woman
Luke 10:38-42

Martha kept house for her brother Lazarus. They were a wealthy family, able to house many visitors under their roof. She and her sister Mary were used to the comings and goings. Jesus and his friends were frequent visitors. It made a lot of work feeding an extra 13 people, but she didn't mind. She had help in the kitchen and there was her sister Mary to ease the burden. The running of the household and the planning of the meals fell to Martha.

Jesus' ministry was primarily to the poor, and his wealthy friends helped to make this possible. They were a well-respected family in the vicinity. Hebrew Law taught that God would prosper those who looked after the needy. And prosper Lazarus he had. Just as well Martha didn't just entertain guests who could invite her back. In the case of Jesus and his friends it would be a fish supper, round a campfire!

Nothing was too much trouble for her, and going into detail to make her guests feel at home was her pride and joy. However, I think she has had a bad press, especially over the incident when Mary left her to it in the kitchen, and went to sit at Jesus' feet.

Martha thought Mary's behaviour was out of order, and not just because she felt she had too much to do. She always had too much to do! Women didn't sit at the feet of the Rabbi. Boys did. Men did. But not women! Everyone knew a woman's place was in the kitchen! Everyone knew that to educate a woman was like casting pearls before swine. Everyone, that is, except Jesus. He didn't seem to notice. So Martha considered it her duty to point it out.

'Lord,' she said, 'don't you care that my sister has left me to do all the work myself? Tell her to help me.'

The Lord answered, 'Martha, Martha, you are worried and upset about many things, but only one thing is needed. Mary has chosen what is better, and it will not be taken away from her.'

What do you think happened next? Do you think Martha flounced off back to the kitchen, slamming the door on the way out? Face like thunder?

I like to think that she wiped her hands on the tea towel, took off her apron and joined Mary at the feet of Jesus. She accepted Jesus' defence of her sister. If it was OK for Mary to be there, it was OK for Martha to be there.

You may remember, after Lazarus died, it seems that Mary went to pieces. But we hear of the ever-active Martha, going about her business. Still feeding people. Still keeping the household going. We are told, when she heard Jesus was coming, she hurried out to meet him, while Mary stayed in the house.

Martha – ever the practical one.

We love to categorise people. For instance, I've said that Martha was the practical one. But when she and Jesus have that wonderful conversation about the resurrection, we begin to realise that she is also is the spiritual one. Jesus reveals truths about himself that so far he has told no one, that he is the Resurrection and the Life.

How Martha loved Mary. She didn't want her to miss any of his wonderful conversation. She hurries back to the house and calls her sister. They both repeat what they had been saying together for days, that if Jesus had been with them, Lazarus would not have died.

I love this picture of Jesus. Strong enough to face up to the Pharisees and teachers of the Law. Strong enough to withstand flogging by the Romans, when many others died. Strong enough to endure the cross, but not afraid to weep openly with his friends. We know the rest of the story: the glorious raising to life of Lazarus.

It comes as no surprise that the last time we hear of Martha, she is serving a wonderful dinner in honour of Jesus.

I think of all the generous, practical people it has been my good fortune to meet, whose motivation is love and service of Jesus.

They are the first to offer hospitality, always there with practical help.

Two such incidents are forever stored in my memory.

When I was in the house alone for the very first time as a young wife, while my husband was in hospital, a friend turned up with her nightdress and stayed for a few days. She came by bus from the next village, knowing I would be lonely. What a practical Christian!

While Claire and I were in hospital whilst she was recovering from an operation, Roy had to go into another hospital at the same time, with very little warning. One phone call was all it needed for a special friend to say yes, she would have Lisa for as long as it took, until we were all back under the same roof.

Both of these friends demonstrated their faith in action.

There are so many opportunities for service within the life of the church. In rural Methodism, many of our meetings would be unattended were it not for generous car drivers!

Being practical is helpful, and it is appreciated, but it isn't enough. We must never neglect what Jesus called 'the better part'. Jesus was essentially a man of the heart, caring deeply about what was going on inside people.

There are times when we need to demonstrate our faith in a practical way. But we also need to sit at the feet of Jesus, to feed on his words. If our relationship with him is right, the practical things fall into place.

The WEALTHY Woman
Luke 8:1-3

Life for Joanna as the wife of Chuza, a high-ranking official in Herod's palace, had never been easy. Lately, it had become impossible. It was hard to keep her integrity, as every day she shared the same space as Herodias and her daughter, Salome. When Herod married Herodias, his brother Philip's wife, John the Baptist denounced the union. She knew it was only a matter of time before they had their revenge. They were wicked, unprincipled people. Her awareness of how bad they were began when she first heard John preach about repentance and God's kingdom. She had an experience of God that left her longing for more.

She had money, position, beautiful clothes and plenty to eat and drink. She had a very comfortable lifestyle. Why, then, did she feel so restless? She thought about the young teacher, Jesus. She had heard him speak lately. The way he behaved towards people filled her with a longing that palace life could not fill. She envied the women in Jesus' group. Mary Magdalene had proved that Jesus had the power to save and to change people. She was not normally Joanna's sort of person but she wanted what Mary had. Peace in her heart. Not the constant struggle to remain faithful to God in this ungodly household. She wanted purpose.

Recently Herod, so excited about his stepdaughter's dancing, promised Salome anything she asked for. Her mother put her up to asking for the head of John the Baptist. Joanna was sickened when Herod fulfilled her wishes. What kind of people would think it entertainment to have someone killed, and their body parts paraded at a party? This, finally, helped Joanna to make up her mind.

Chuza and everyone in the palace knew she was interested in this 'new' faith. Even Chuza's position had been threatened because of it. But her wealth and position seemed empty, worthless. So finally she left, and became one of Jesus' disciples.

Then her real life began. She was included in the group, listening closely to every word of Jesus, and her tasks now were so different. Helping the crowds that seemed permanently to surround Jesus. Making a 'home' wherever Jesus and his followers were. She was fulfilled as never before.

No excitement in the palace had ever matched Jesus' entry into Jerusalem. The crowds cheek by jowl in the streets. The sound was deafening. Everyone caught the mood. Being part of it, her heart swelled with pride. Jesus deserved this, for all his work of healing, raising the dead, giving sight to blind people, preaching such good news, especially to the poor. Finally people were getting the message! She had known it for some time herself, but now the secret was out! Jesus was the promised Messiah. She waved branches and called out just as loudly as anyone. What a fantastic day! What a fantastic experience!

She had hoped the euphoria would last more than a day! But it was not to be. Not everyone shared her enthusiasm. The Pharisees and the Teachers of the Law were not impressed. Jesus didn't endear himself to the Temple staff either, when he started upturning tables and chasing out money-changers. Sure, she understood him; he had spoken about hypocrisy so many times in the past.

How he suffered after his arrest, and how she loved him. The so-called 'trial', the roughing up by the soldiers, the flogging and then the crucifixion. She was never far away in those dark days.

But then, the greatest moment in her life, worth anything she had given up, was to know the amazing truth that Jesus was alive, and he had entrusted his women friends to take the news to his disciples. Joanna hugged to herself the knowledge that Jesus trusted her with this incredible news. No matter what the world did, how vile and wicked it was, it could not defeat Jesus! God had raised him up. All the things he had said about his death and resurrection were true! He had proved it. She had seen for herself. Jesus had said that no one who leaves home and a settled life to follow him will go unrewarded. Not necessarily in this life, but in the next. Her opportunities to serve Jesus continued. Whatever she did for others, she knew she was doing for Jesus. Even a cup of cold water, given in his name, was given for him. And she knew for certain that this life was not the end, that God would raise her up too and, because of Jesus' death, she would be able to walk boldly up to God's throne. She never hankered after the palace she had lived in and left, but she looked forward to seeing Jesus again.

She remembered the sweet fellowship with him and his friends, both men and women. Under the stars, along the dusty roads, the men would come back to the camp, excited and tired. Exhilarated and dusty. The talk would go on long into the night. The laughter, and prayers, the full-hearted singing. The good-humoured teasing. The shared meals. And most of all Jesus. She pictured the joy, when he gave health and new life to sick people, forgiveness and hope to the defeated.

Ah, Jesus!

You may think I have used a little too much poetic licence here. OK. It's an opinion.

How do I know that Jesus would be full of joy when he ministered to others? I'll tell you.

In the last 10 years I have been nine times to Kenya, once to South Africa, once to Ghana, and to Bangladesh. Every time I have travelled, very kind people have given me money to give away. Can you imagine what it's like for me to be 'Lady Bountiful'? I have never earned much. In fact I was only employed for 10 years of my life. The rest of the time I have been a home-maker. Then I was self-employed, running a Fair Trade shop for over 11 years. The most I paid myself was £40 a week. Now as a flat-rate pensioner I am receiving more in my own right than ever before! (£45.20.) Fortunately I have been a 'kept' woman: kept by my husband Roy and the provision of God.

Over the years, on behalf of others, I have sunk a bore-well in the Ngong Hills in Kenya, provided two diesel generators, an industrial washing machine, a photocopier in a special-needs school in Nairobi, glass for school windows and many other things. Other people have supplied the money, but I have been the one witnessing the difference these gifts make. I am the one who has witnessed the joy with which these gifts have been received.

I'll tell you about one such gift.

I once went on an incredible trip to Bangladesh to visit the Revd John Hastings and his lovely wife, and dear friend of mine, Joyce. I was visiting 'Nijera Shikhi,' a mass education programme devised by John and supported by the Methodist Church. Most of the fare was paid by my friends in the East Anglia District of the Church.

I stayed with John and Joyce in their flat in Shyamoli, in downtown Dhaka, Bangladesh. I will never forget the impact of nine million people, most of whom seem to have been on the streets at the same time! It was a real contrast when we travelled miles out into the countryside, along the raised narrow paths between the rice paddies, in a two-stroke 'baby taxi'. Long-legged John, Joyce and I tucked in behind the driver. We visited one of the women's groups participating in the literacy programme. We met in a clay lump house and all sat on a shiny dirt floor, John in the middle, surrounded by brightly dressed mothers with several babies. John spoke in fluent Bengali. Suddenly they all clapped. Unable to understand what they were saying, I asked Joyce what John had said. He had been telling them about me, and how I had come to Bangladesh to learn about Nijera Shikhi, to go home and promote the work in the UK. They clapped because he had told them I had provided them with a community library. These people were very poor, and could never imagine owning a library of their own. Their joy was undisguised. So was mine. In fact a great smile spreads across my face just to remember it. The library cost £21 and the money was given to me by one of my most generous friends, to spend on her behalf. This was just one of the many projects 'I' have been able to support. Though others have supplied the means, I have been the one 'up front', seeing the faces, sharing the joy.

That's how I know that Jesus would be full of joy. Because I was full of joy!

The willingness to go there had come from me, but everything else had come from God, through my friends. Imagine the joy Jesus experienced whenever he healed, or raised someone. For the joy set before him, Jesus endured the cross, gave his life for us.

Perhaps at this moment, you are tempted to hug your life to yourself. To look at your possessions and the comfort of your home and say No when God calls you to do something beautiful for him.

Take a long, long look at Jesus. When you turn back and look at all the things that hinder your service, you will see that, compared to him, they are dust and ashes.

Kick the door open wide and follow him.

The WORKING Woman
Matthew 8:14-18

She looked at her hands. How strange, they looked just like her mother's! She remembered her Mum's lined face, always beautiful in her daughter's eyes. Her hands folded neatly in her lap. Fast asleep with her sewing on the floor, where it had slipped as she had nodded off.

Whatever is wrong with me today, she said to herself. I haven't got time for dreaming. Mother's been gone for years. It was just that, as she sat down wearily for a moment and her eyes rested on her own hands, the memories came flooding back. Tears stung her eyes, and she longed for the caress and comfort that her mother's hands had always brought her. I'm tired, that's what's wrong with me. I'll just have a few minutes then I'll carry on. She couldn't spare any time off today, of all days.

She had worked hard all her life, but didn't mind a bit. Coming from a rural fishing community, indeed, she had never expected anything else. When she had married and had her own little home, she took such pride in her hospitality. Proud of her Jewish traditions, she was a good cook, loved to go down to the market and pick out her own produce. Experimenting with herbs and spices. Making a little go a long way. There was an ever-open door, which was just as well. As the children grew up, they delighted in having their friends round. Feeding them up was her greatest pleasure.

When her husband died, she had gone to live with one of her daughters, who had married a local fisherman called Peter.

She would not deny that she had been a bit shocked when Peter announced that he was leaving his fishing, and was going to become a disciple of Jesus. She was shocked, yet not surprised. They had all heard Jesus talk, they had been won over by his joyous love of life and the genuine goodness that flowed out of him, witnessing for themselves Jesus' power to heal, and to make God so real.

No, she wasn't surprised. She had been anxious at first for her daughter, of course, but 'Jehovah Jireh', God will provide. And he had. Peter had been back, when he was in Capernaum, keeping them up to date with his adventures. Thrilling them with tales of feeding massive crowds, of blind people receiving their sight, even of lepers being cleansed. Fancy Jesus touching lepers! She looked down again at her own hands. No, I don't think I could do that. But I had better do something soon. They would all be here tomorrow. Peter had invited Jesus and all his friends to the house.

It's hot in here.

She slept. Waking fitfully, she thought of lying beside still waters, the deep pool spoken of by King David. She realised she was wet with sweat. But she was too tired to stir herself. So very tired. Her daughter's face floated in front of her eyes. Why didn't they leave her alone? All she wanted to do was sleep. To think again of that cool refreshing pool. She had no idea how long she lay there, hovering between life and death.

There was a commotion. Noise and movement. She opened her eyes. The pool with the still water was gone! Instead there was a beautiful face, weathered by the sun and wind. Brilliant eyes looking into hers with such intensity. Ah! Jesus!

Oh, that's right, he's coming for a meal. She leapt up. They'd never manage all that food without her. To her surprise the room burst with good-humoured laughter and shouts of praise. What was everybody doing? She had no idea, but she joined in. She felt great!

It came as a big surprise to hear that she had been so ill. She had no idea that Jesus had healed her. When she did know, she wanted to serve him, to wait on him, fatten him up, like only a Jewish mother knew how . . .

I come from a hard-working family. A non-church family. My dad was a fine man, with a very strong work ethic. I lived in a large house that always had room for one more. Some of the evacuees who came to live with us during the war moved out when we did in 1961! I guess it made sense then, when I fell in love, that it would be with a self-employed builder and plumber. We married in 1963 and moved to Norfolk in 1964. Our home, too, has been an open house, given to hospitality. I have always worked, but not very often in paid employment!

When I became a Christian, I wanted to serve Jesus. And no matter how many times I talk to myself before I go to a meeting, very often when volunteers are being asked for I hear this voice saying yes! And realise it's me!

No complaints.

The first women's meeting I went to was in 1964 at Harleston Congregational church. At the age of 22 I was the youngest. But I absolutely loved it. I met so many women like the one in the story I've just told. So hard-working and generous. We loved our singing, baking and craft-making, and each other's company. I first became a speaker at that meeting. I am truly grateful for their confidence in me, and their encouragement has been a great blessing.

As the years went on I became a Methodist, joining the Women's Fellowship at Pulham Market, and then at Diss. I love our District meetings, and have become well known locally over the years as the 'Traidcraft Lady'.

I would like to celebrate for a few minutes the hard-working women I have known. Freely giving of their time and energy. Unstinting with their service, sharing their talents, skills and graces. I have been fortunate to know some of the most affectionate, generous and loving people. I know them as Margaret, Betty, Laurine, Ann, Jean and Maggie. Ruby, Winnie, Cathy, Marjorie, Alice and Doreen. Dora, Daisy, Greta, Ivy, Connie and Edna. Helen, Maureen, Lorna and Eileen. And so many, many more.

Your list will be different from mine. Different names, different women, but the same wonderful qualities.

Perhaps you would like to spend a moment looking at your own hands, thinking about the work you've achieved with them, and remembering some of the wonderful Jesus Women in your own life.

The PROMISCUOUS Woman
John 8:2-11

It was very early in the morning. Before daybreak, and they were still in bed. She awoke with a start. Her lover's face was a silhouette in the gloom. There was a thundering on the door again. She leapt from the bed and hastily slipped her arms into her thin robe as she headed towards the noise. As she drew back the bolts, the door burst open beneath her hands.

A Teacher of the Law from the Temple grabbed her wrist in a vice-like grip. 'You slut,' he hissed. 'Come with me.' She shot a glance back to the bed, where her lover sat bolt upright, eyes wide open in fear. He didn't move.

She was on her own!

The early morning cold chilled her near-naked body as she was dragged along the streets. Other Teachers and a crowd began to follow them. The grip on her wrist tightened as her captor dragged her through the people to the Temple Courts and flung her against the wall. She stayed upright, her wild hair framing her terrified face. To be confronted by – Jesus.

Does this sound like a bodice-ripping yarn from a cheap novel? It surely does.

Every story, every meeting, every confrontation we read about in the Gospels, was with real people. Remember that. When we read about Jesus' reaction, remember he was looking at a real person.

The atmosphere was electric. This was not about the woman. This was all about trapping Jesus. She was just a pawn in the Pharisees' game. There were plenty of women doing what she was doing. But she was the one they knew about and decided to use. This was no spur-of-the-moment decision. The Teachers of God's Law, so often ignoring the Law themselves, didn't care who they used, so long as they trapped Jesus. They were desperate to have a basis for accusing him.

'Teacher,' they said 'this woman was caught in the act of adultery. In the Law of Moses, God commanded us to stone such a woman. Now, what do you say?'

Terrified, the woman dropped to her knees, bracing herself for the first stone.

Nothing happened.

There was silence. She looked up and Jesus was writing something in the dust with his finger.

In spite of the early morning cold, she was sweating.

Then the questions flew fast and furious, and the noise increased, as they kept on and on . . .

Eventually Jesus straightened up. The crowd was stilled as they waited for his answer.

Jesus said, 'If any one of you is without sin, let him be the first to throw a stone at her.'

Then he bent down and wrote some more.

One by one, the men peeled away. First some of the old men, their eyes downcast, then all of them, including her accusers. Finally she and Jesus had the place to themselves.

Jesus straightened up and looked around. Then his eyes turned back to her. 'Woman, where are they? Has no one condemned you?'

'No one, sir,' she said.

'Then neither do I condemn you,' Jesus declared. 'Go now and leave your life of sin.'

This story renders me speechless. Well, nearly.

It is so beautiful!

So human!

So Divine!

So Jesus!

The WITTY Woman
Matthew 15:21-28

Coming from Syrian-occupied Phoenicia to live in Tyre, she had learned to hold her own with anybody! As a Greek woman with a disabled child in an alien community, she had developed a strong personality.

She loved her vulnerable daughter so much, seeing the real person trapped inside her little body. Knowing she was powerless to release her lovely child, she prayed constantly. It didn't matter to whose god she prayed. The God of the Jews would do. She knew a fair bit about them all!

When she heard about Jesus, newly arrived from Jerusalem, capital of the Jewish Faith, she went in search of him. Rumour said he healed anyone and everyone, beggars and rich men alike. She wondered how he felt about foreigners. She would soon find out.

Unable to get close to him, she kept crying out. 'Lord, Son of David, have mercy on me.' She wasn't a Jew, but she knew their scriptures. Maybe, if she sounded orthodox he would turn round and speak to her. She realised she was getting louder by his disciples' reaction, but she was desperate.

'Lord, Son of David, have mercy on me. My daughter endures terrible suffering from demon possession.'

Not a word! But she was encouraged. Jesus didn't send her away as his friends suggested. She confronted him, her eyes blazing out of a flushed face.

His answer took the wind out of her sails and brought her to her knees.

'I was sent only to the lost sheep of Israel,' he said. Was he challenging her use of his scriptures!

But it didn't put her off. 'Lord, help me,' she said.

Jesus gently replied, 'It is not right to take the children's bread and toss it to their dogs.'

She thought quickly. 'Even the dogs eat the crumbs that fall from their master's table.'

Jesus liked her answer. She could tell by the smile around his mouth as they eyed each other up. With their gaze locked, he said: 'Woman, you have great faith. Your request is granted.'

Looking back she realised she should have stopped to thank him. But she fled immediately to her daughter, wanting to see if his words were true. There, lying on the bed, no longer trapped in her poor body, but fit and well, was the girl she had always known was there. Healed by Jesus.

This woman, because of her past experiences, had developed this tough shell and ready wit. Look how it paid off for her that day!

The influences that shape our lives are strange things.

When I was a girl, my mum used to say, 'You will never be beautiful like your sister.' Being beautiful was important to Mum, a very good-looking woman. I guess that's why I developed my personality more than my looks! Having a quick wit, even at an early age, meant I was often surrounded by laughter. Sometimes my boss at the Rates Office would remind me that we worked in a public building, not at a Vaudeville theatre!

Because I so often felt I didn't measure up to my mother's standards, as I grew up I would hear a little whisper in my head: 'You won't be able to do this.' My standard answer used to be, 'Just you watch me!'

Discovering that Jesus loves me unconditionally blew all the doubts away. Well, most of them. The mercy and grace of God sees me as beautiful in Jesus. Unblemished and very presentable!

Is your confidence at a low ebb? Be bold! It's you whom Jesus loves. In Christ Jesus we are a unique combination of God and ourselves, referred to as the treasure in the earthen pots. No matter what the exterior, the contents are of enormous value, worth the Son of God leaving the splendour of heaven, to live on earth and die for.

Be yourself in Jesus.

The RECKLESS Woman
Luke 21:1-4

She knew that the Teachers of the Law in their showy robes liked to be seen around town, being 'holy'. How they loved the places of honour at banquets, and the most important seats in the synagogue. She was aware that they exploited their position for their own gain, very often at the expense of widows like her.

They were welcome to it! She wouldn't swap with them. She hated being 'up the front'. She never minded how far back she stood. She came in through the Gate of the Women. Since she had become a widow, she was totally reliant on her family to support her. She struggled, there was no doubt about it. Making ends meet had never been easy, even when her husband was alive.

But she had her dignity, and above all she had her faith. Occasionally, with careful budgeting, she would have a surplus. Like today. She had two small copper coins. She had no idea what would come her way next week, but today she had two coins over! She knew exactly what she wanted to do with them.

It grieved her that most of the time she couldn't make her offering to God. But today was different. Her money was as good as the next person's, it was hers to give, and she was going to give it.

Being a Jewish woman, identified with Sarah, Rachel, Hannah and all the great women in her history, she just wanted to honour God. She wanted to show him how much she valued him.

The money wasn't for the Teachers of the Law.

It wasn't even to support the Temple, much as she loved it.

It was for God.

She didn't see the finely dressed men and women pouring large amounts into the Temple treasury. She was only aware of herself as she climbed the steps and threw her money into the great golden trumpet. Unsurprisingly, the coins made no noise as they fell into the coffer at the bottom. She didn't see the new Rabbi Jesus sitting opposite with his friends. She kept her head down, knowing that only the most senior Rabbis were allowed to teach in the treasury. She had no idea she was being observed. She was only concerned for God to know.

She tossed the coins in. There, she felt human again; she was able to hold her head up, because she had been able to give!

Then she turned away and walked off into obscurity.

No, she didn't.

Two thousand years later I've just told a little of her story. God did see her, and her gift, through the eyes of Jesus.

His disciples had been watching pop-eyed! The amount of money being thrown into the treasury was a pretty impressive sight. They felt like country yokels compared to the wealth and sophistication of the Temple.

Jesus beckoned his disciples to him, indicating the fast-disappearing back of the widow and said: 'I tell you the truth, this poor widow has put more into the treasury than all the others. They all gave out of their wealth, but she, out of her poverty, put in everything – all she had to live on.'

We have no idea how revolutionary this teaching of Jesus was! Strict codes governed all the activities in the Temple. Money from the rich and powerful really counted for something. Coming in through that Gate of the Pure and Just was like belonging to some exclusive club. They had been taught that God prospered the Pure and the Just. That's why they were rich and powerful. Yet Jesus is praising this poor widow! It was not what the disciples were used to hearing!

What are we to make of Jesus' words? I have heard this interpreted as 'every little helps'. I'm sure it does. But I don't think this is what Jesus is teaching here.

The value placed by God on this gift has got nothing to do with the amount. It has everything to do with the heart.

He was saying, you haven't given as much as she has given, till you've given all you've got.

As Christians, God has access to our hearts. He knows all about us. Our giving, and our self-indulgence.

It has been said that if God has the person, he has the purse. I guess it's about how we value God and what he has done for us.

Not all giving, though, can be measured in financial terms.

One of my favourite people, of the many who have passed though my life, was Mrs Froud.

I didn't know her until she was elderly, yet when I looked into her eyes I could see the girl she still was on the inside. She was the Deacon appointed to look after me when I was baptised by immersion. She became one of my most valued friends.

When Mrs Froud was a young wife, she saw a poster advertising a Mission at Diss Baptist Church. She was not a churchgoer, but decided to go to one of the meetings. The preacher presented Jesus and his love, and told his congregation that he wanted them to fall in love with Jesus as they had fallen in love with their partners. As a young wife this was significant to her, but Mrs Froud thought that it was nonsense! But she came back for more, and before the Mission was over she had indeed fallen in love with Jesus. That 'love affair' lasted all her life.

It got her into all sorts of trouble with her husband! He told her she would have to choose between him and the church. When she decided to be baptised he put her clothes in a suitcase and left it outside, told her he didn't want her in the house. Once he found a card among her belongings which said: 'I will never leave you, or forsake you.' Not knowing these were the words of Jesus he accused her of 'carrying on with the Pastor'! Mrs Froud weathered all these storms. Her faith was as vibrant when I knew her as it was when she was a young woman. Many, many years later as a widow, Mrs Froud did not sleep in her own bed, but every night she went and slept in the home of a disabled woman, so that this lady could stay in her own home. She gave, and gave, and gave again.

She went to be with the Lord many years ago, but her memory to me is fresh and vital. She is one of the many people I look forward to seeing again in 'My Father's house'.

What is it that 'demands my soul, my life, my all'? Isaac Watts said that it's the 'love so amazing, so divine' that Jesus showed us on the cross.

Do we need to look again at Jesus, and his life given for us? What would ever be enough to give to him?

Jesus' teaching on giving was revolutionary!

Join the revolution!

The CONSTANT Woman
John 2:1-11

The Jesus Woman with the largest role is Mary, his mother.

Her story is one of faith, obedience, goodness and constancy. From conception to crucifixion, from domesticity to dusty roads and danger. In all of these, Mary was constant.

Seeing these qualities in advance, God chose her to be the mother of his Son, Jesus. A faithful Jewish girl, young and pure in heart. When her fiancé Joseph found she was pregnant, he loved her so much he didn't want to expose her shame publicly. Joseph, though hurt himself, was unwilling to hurt her. What joy for him to know she hadn't been sleeping around. God had made her pregnant! OK! He knew how that sounded, that's why he didn't tell anybody! It was their first shared secret. There were many more to come.

It was never easy, that's for sure. From the disappointment at the beginning, and the first of his powerful dreams from God, Joseph sensed he was in for a bumpy ride.

Mary treasured up many things in her heart. Surely she took those thoughts and memories out from time to time to re-examine them!

The extraordinary birth among strangers in Bethlehem.

The rough surroundings, and the strange visitors.

When a group of local shepherds came to see the baby, she was too tired and happy with her new son to worry about privacy.

Would she ever forget the Mystery Men with the symbolic gifts?

Fleeing in fear from her homeland into Egypt?

Being a refugee?

All the while hugging her secret to herself, that her son Jesus was God's Son.

As he grew, Jesus filled her heart with praise. He was so full of life and joy! Exuberant and witty, gregarious and loving. Studious and willing to learn. Not just the scriptures, but the skills Joseph taught him. It was just as well he did, for when Joseph died Jesus became the breadwinner, until his brothers were old enough to help. He was fit and attractive, strong and hard-working, good at dealing with the customers.

Mary knew that one day all this domestic happiness had to come to an end. Jesus would be moving on when the time was right. Those early years and the sure knowledge that he was God's own Son told her that. She knew he would be a great leader and teacher. Recently he had been baptised by his cousin, John, and had started to draw a group of fine young men to him.

When the family was invited to a wedding in Cana, they were embarrassed for the host when the wine started to run out before the celebrations were thoroughly under way. Because she had no idea when Jesus' ministry would begin, she was pushing her luck when she went to Jesus, confident he would be able to do something. He good-humouredly put his hands either side of her face and said, 'Dear woman, why do you involve me? My time has not yet come.' Was this some kind of signal? Was Mary telling Jesus, I know that you are more than special? I know that you must leave the family and me. That what you have belongs on a wider stage. Did they look at each other for a long time while this message was communicated? Because, in spite of what Jesus had said, Mary said to the servants, 'Do whatever he tells you.'

I love this story of Jesus' first miracle. The servants filled the stone jars with water and when they poured them out, they were full of fine wine! No one other than Mary, Jesus and the servants knew where this special wine had come from.

You may have a problem with miracles. Some Christians believe that because God was not restricted to time, he was able to speed up the process needed to produce what would usually take months, into an instant. But he needed the basic ingredients!

For example, at the wedding, he needed the water to turn it into wine. For the feeding of the 5,000, he needed the bread and the fish. In the healings, he needed to be confronted with sickness, not necessarily physically, as some of the healings were from a distance.

It seems he needs the raw materials.

I don't have a problem with miracles, but what I have had a struggle with has been putting the 'raw materials' into his hands. When I have turned myself, and whatever confronts me over to him, Jesus has turned my water into wine.

You would think that with so many blessings in my life, I would never be hesitant or reluctant. The longer I have known him, the easier it should have become. Perhaps I am what is called a 'practising Christian'? Needing more practice than most! Usually, the more you do something, the easier it gets.

This is not always true about our dealings with Jesus.

It is temping to hang on, and not hand over.

Looking at the healing miracles of Jesus, convinced as I am that he is the same today as he was then, I confess I am stumped! He could have healed my ovaries years ago, given me the natural family I so longed for. But if he had I would not have known Claire and Lisa. Trouble is, if you change one thing, you change everything!

If there had been a great shaft of light from heaven and God had answered all my prayers back in 1964, I would have missed some of the most beautiful people I've known. Being involved with men, women and children with disabilities has enriched my life.

Working at a local Special Needs School has brought our daughter Lisa enormous satisfaction.

From the dizzy heights of 'now', I would not change a thing.

I wouldn't swap this living water for all the wine in Cana!

Wherever you are at this moment, whatever you are confronted with, hand over the raw materials to God.

Don't leave Jesus out of the equation.

The DELIGHTED Woman
Matthew 9:18-26

She knew she was being unreasonable, but her helplessness made her crazy. Now was not the time to weigh up the pros and cons of contacting Jesus. Surely Jairus could see that their daughter was slipping further into a coma? What did synagogue politics matter at a time like this? She continued to bathe the white face of her beautiful child, tears running unchecked down her cheeks.

Frustration made her bold.

'I know you're a synagogue leader and you're not supposed to admire this Jesus. But for God's sake, man, you've seen him heal the sick. Go and fetch him!'

Jairus looked back one more time at his beloved women folk, then sped out of the door.

Jesus was easy to find. Jairus just followed the crowd, and there he was!

He wasted no time. Inhibitions gone, he fell at Jesus' feet and said, 'My daughter's dying. Please come and put your hands on her, so that she will be healed and live.'

Jesus turned immediately and went with him. There was a brief wait as Jesus had a conversation with a woman in the crowd.

As Jairus, Jesus and his friends were nearing the house, the worst happened. Men from the house met them. 'Your daughter's dead,' they told Jarius brutally. 'Why bother the Teacher any more?'

Were they secretly relieved, these bearers of bad news? Relieved that there wouldn't be an 'incident' with Jesus and they needn't have to appear to be among his supporters?

Jairus' wife knew her daughter had gone. The noise of wailing insulted her ears. Where had these people come from? What was all this row?

She looked up as Jesus entered the room.

His fine face was serene. Was that a hint of a smile round his lips?

'Why all this commotion and wailing?' The smile widened. 'The child is not dead but asleep.'

The house rang with laughter. Derisive laughter.

Her heart, which minutes before had felt like a stone, quickened.

Jesus took Jairus, the girl's mother, Peter, James and John into the inner room.

Kneeling on the floor, Jesus held her daughter's hand and said, 'Little girl, I say to you, get up.'

We could not possibly imagine the contrasts of that occasion!

Wailing and commotion in the outer room.

Peace and joy in the child's bedroom.

We are told they were completely astonished! An understatement, I would suggest. It's hard for us to imagine the impact of this 12 year old girl walking through the noisy crowd into the kitchen for something to eat!

I'd loved to have seen their faces.

The astonished crowd, the weeping father, the delighted mother. Jesus full of joy.

There was more going on here than a simple healing, (as if Jesus healings were ever simple!).

This man was a synagogue leader. If we are familiar with the Gospels, we are left in no doubt about what the leaders of the synagogues thought of Jesus. They helped to bring about his death, charging him with blasphemy. The real charge, though, was his radical challenge to their thinking and their interpretation of God's Law.

This man Jairus was already different. Witness his love for his wife and for his daughter.

Generally, religious leaders did not value women. But this man did.

Generally, religious leaders did not value Jesus and his teaching. This man did.

Generally, religious leaders did not kneel at the feet of Jesus. This man did.

Jairus had seen enough of Jesus to know that he valued women.

He knew Jesus would not hesitate to come to his daughter.

Faith, grown from desperation, gave him back his family.

I love the way Matthew brings this story together with the woman who had the haemorrhage. The woman had suffered for 12 years with no hope of a normal relationship or of having a family. The Jairus family had only one daughter in a society that valued sons. When the daughter was born 12 years before, this woman first began to haemorrhage.

This day, when she reached out her hand to touch Jesus, her new life began.

This day, when Jesus reached out his hand to hold the hand of the girl, her new life began. It is inconceivable to me (no pun intended) that with the stopping of the bleeding, this woman would not have had a 'normal' life. As a Jewish woman, her heart's desire was a husband, a home, children.

Whenever I travel in Africa, I always take some photos of my family. Many's the time women will look at the family group, see that we have two daughters, and say, 'Doesn't your husband mind?'

I delight in telling them that we value girls.

Then they notice that Claire is disabled.

Again the same question: 'Doesn't your husband mind?'

I delight in telling them that we value Claire, just as she is.

Do we value women, as much as Jesus does?

Do we affirm and encourage each other to share the ministry of Jesus today?

Are children welcome in our churches?

Do we make provision for exuberant teenagers?

Do we make allowances for people to be 'different'?

If we are struggling with the answers to these questions, remember that the same Jesus lives in us today, through his Holy Spirit.

As he was a substitute for us on the cross for our forgiveness, he can be a substitute for us for our deliverance from prejudice and intolerance.

Too tricky to understand?

Just say by faith, 'Lord, I'm getting it wrong. Heal my attitudes and make me more like you.'

The WASTEFUL Woman
John 12:1-11

No one spoke about waste, when the sumptuous meals were being served! Lavish food and wine. It was fine while money was being spent on *all* of them. Yet on that one occasion, when Mary broke the jar of expensive perfume for Jesus alone, it was considered wasteful! Not just by Judas, but by the others too. Mary knew it wasn't wasted on Jesus. She was confident he knew what was in her heart.

'Why are you troubling her?' he asked.

It wasn't the first time Jesus had defended her in front of the guests. On the first occasion there was food and drink, bustle in the kitchen. Mary helped with the preparation as was expected of her. But as soon as she was free, she left the chores and joined the men where Jesus was teaching. It took courage to walk past her brother and his friends to sit at Jesus' feet. It wasn't a woman's business. Even Martha, her dear sister, chose not to understand, asking Jesus to send Mary back to the domestic chores. She remembered with joy Jesus' reaction. He defended her right to be there. He defended her right to education and he acknowledged her spirituality. She knew he would, and it had given her courage. Later others began to recognise the different-ness of Jesus and his attitude to women. But she was one of the first. No wonder she loved him!

Her world was torn apart when Lazarus became ill. The sisters sent a message immediately to Jesus, never doubting that he would come and make their dear brother well again. They knew how much Jesus loved them all, that he knew that if anything happened to Lazarus, they would be unprotected in this male dominated society.

He didn't come.

Why had he let them down?

Again the house was full. This time people were offering condolences for their loss. Even the visitors from Jerusalem were saying, 'After all the other healings you would have expected him to heal his friend.' Mary hated the criticism. But the truth had to be faced. Lazarus was dead, and Jesus wasn't there.

So deep was Mary's grief, she didn't notice her sister leave the house. But when Martha returned with the news that Jesus had arrived, she got up immediately and hurried out with her. Her departure was so hurried that the rest of the mourners got up to follow her. She knew they meant well, that they cared about her and wanted to comfort her. But how she longed to speak to Jesus alone!

As soon as she saw him she said, 'If you had been here my brother would not have died.'

Jesus' face crumpled and he too wept. There had been so many tears that day.

But tears had turned to laughter! Pain had turned to joy. Jesus proved he was the Resurrection and the Life, by raising Lazarus from death. The wake turned into a wedding banquet! Mary smiled, remembering. Lazarus' family and friends were overjoyed, and many people came just to stare at him.

But not everyone was happy.

The Jewish leaders were plotting to kill Jesus and, some said, her brother too.

The family threw a party to celebrate Lazarus' new life. It was seriously lavish! This time they really had something to celebrate.

It was after the meal, as everyone was sitting round talking, that Mary brought out her present. It never crossed her mind that it would be seen as too costly, too generous, especially under the circumstances.

Hearing the rumours about the future, Mary suspected that this could be the last thing she would do for Jesus. She knew he would understand the symbolism as she broke the jar of perfume and poured it onto his feet. She thought of Psalm 133: 'How very good and pleasant it is when kindred live together in unity! It is like precious oil on the head, running down over the collar of his robes. It is like the dew of Hermon, which flows on the mountains of Mount Zion. For there the Lord ordained his blessing, life for evermore.'

Jesus had treated her like a beloved sister. Though others criticised, she knew that between her and Jesus there was unity.

Judas and the other disciples asked, 'Why this waste?'

Strangely, it didn't seem like waste to Mary. It was a response to Jesus. How much would ever be enough to express what was in her full heart? The fragrance of the perfume filled the house, clung to Jesus' clothes. As the soldiers divided those clothes a few days later, did they detect the sweet fragrance? While he was alive, Mary anointed his body for death. A few days later Jesus was dead. When the women went early to the tomb, it was empty.

Mary did what she could, when she could.

I remember a time when someone said to me, 'What a waste!'

Shortly after we had taken a little Downs syndrome baby into our lives, I was taking an anniversary service in a local church. Enjoying the service, a member of the congregation said admiringly, 'Are you a teacher?'

'I'm a foster-parent.'

'How many children do you have?'

'Just one child with Downs syndrome.'

'What a waste!' she said.

Momentarily I was crushed. Then I experienced what I can only describe as 'the Spirit of Glory', an awareness that I was right in the centre of God's will for me. I realised I would rather be 'wasted' on God than do anything else with my life.

A life lived in joy for him is never wasted. Kingdom values are not easy to understand. The first shall be last, and the last shall be first.

Claire is 31 now. She is a great influence in my life. Every day is a fresh new beginning. She never brings any of the petty hurts and resentments of yesterday into today. I have learned much through Claire's faith and witness. She is my 'secret weapon'.

When she was much younger and did something 'wrong', I taught her to say she was sorry, and then it would be forgiven and done with. So if I mentioned the matter again, she would say with great indignation, 'I have apologised!'

She meant, how could I possibly bring this up again when it had already been dealt with? What a lesson about God and his forgiveness!

Mary did what she could, when she had the chance to.

Be wasteful. Give everything you are and everything you have to Jesus. Now, while you have a chance.

Lord, let not my life be full of regret for things undone for you.

The ENABLED Woman
Luke 13:10-17

She had spent a lot of time thinking about the relationship between sins and suffering. This was not an academic question to keep her brain active. This was a genuine attempt to understand what had happened to her. She was bent double with a severe curvature of the spine. For 18 years she had not felt the sun on her face, or looked into the eyes of her loved ones.

Yet she was not embittered. She couldn't understand why God was punishing her as the Teachers of the Law taught. Every Saturday she could be found in the synagogue, in the place reserved for women, listening intently to the scriptures being read and interpreted. She was well-known, being so easily recognisable. Mercifully, because she was so disabled by her bent back, she was spared the pitying looks of her fellow worshippers.

This Sabbath, there was a new teacher.

Suddenly into her eye-line appeared masculine, sandalled feet. She heard the teacher say: 'Woman, you are set free from your infirmity', as gentle hands helped her to unbend. For the first time in 18 years she stood at her full height, and looked straight into the eyes of her healer. Jesus' eyes were full of love and empathy. She immediately began praising God, knowing, without any shadow of doubt, that this healing was a gift from him.

The people round her were delighted. They were thrilled with Jesus.

So it was a shock when the synagogue leader looked at her with distaste and said: 'There are six days for work. So come and be healed on those days and not the Sabbath.'

If that was meant as a put-down, it didn't work! She was drinking in the sights, the faces of her neighbours not seen for years, and this lovely young teacher with his radiant face and loving eyes.

Then he said something so breathtaking that the shock was tangible!

'You hypocrites! Does not each of you on the Sabbath untie his ox or his donkey from the manger, and lead it away to give it water? And ought not this woman, a daughter of Abraham whom Satan bound for 18 long years, be set free from this bondage on the Sabbath day?'

This daughter of Abraham! No wonder all the men were in shock! No one had ever said such a thing. They were all sons of Abraham, but a daughter of Abraham? A daughter of faith? A woman equal with a man?

Not only was Jesus saying that this woman was more important than the Sabbath.

Not only was Jesus saying that this woman was more important than one of their donkeys or oxen.

But he was actually saying that Abraham had daughters in the Faith. That God treated them with equal dignity and honour, that their value was the same in the sight of God.

If you have ever been in doubt about the radical teachings of Jesus, consider this. Standing in the synagogue surrounded by the Teachers of the Law and the men who considered themselves so superior to their women folk, Jesus paid women the highest compliment. He affirmed this woman's faith and cared about her suffering. We talk today of the 'holistic approach'. Jesus was there first!

His opponents were humiliated.

The people were delighted.

The disabled woman was enabled.

Enabled to live a full life. Delivered by Jesus to grow in her faith.

No wonder plain people loved him.

No wonder the Teachers hated him.

Because of the strict codes in the synagogue, Jesus had to cross from where he was to where this woman was. He could go to where she stood, but she could not go to him. Jesus took the initiative. With genuine love for this woman, knowing that he would alienate the Teachers of the Law, Jesus crossed that divide. All these things contributed to his trial and his death. But he was set on a mission of Divine love. Nothing and nobody would stand in his way, until he had endured the cross.

Why? For joy! For the joy of bringing us to God.

Jesus still sets people free. Jesus still enables people.

I could tell you how Jesus delivered me from a bad temper, or from dependence on all sorts of things. But the real testimony would have to come from the people I live with and can vouch for the truth of that deliverance!

So I will tell you about a violent rapist, who had been dependent on heroin, delivered by Jesus from drugs and violence. I met him when I was a prison visitor. He was a 'lifer' and had served 14 years of his sentence when I first met him. He was a man who had known no love or affection in his life, turned out of home at an early age, and handed from one person to another. He had never had a reasonable relationship with a woman, and in fact he had no idea that it was possible to have such a thing. All women to him were, in his own words, 'slags'.

The key to his deliverance was a Christian lady visitor who came into his life. She visited weekly, building up a relationship out of his bitterness and hatred, looking beyond the rejection, pain and prejudice. Gradually they became friends and she was able to introduce him to Jesus. Through this 'normal' relationship with his visitor he started to value women for the first time in his life. A turning point came for this man when his visitor was able to embrace him with genuine acceptance. Once he was free of his heroin addiction he was able to become what God had intended him to be.

He was a very good musician, and I used to send him some sheet music into prison to practise, and then he would accompany my singing on the following Sunday.

Rightly or wrongly we always took Claire with us to the Prison Fellowship meetings. Claire doesn't judge people. She doesn't see 'an old lag', or 'violent scum', she just takes people at face value. One Sunday as I was leading the fellowship I used something Claire had done during the week as an example. Claire, pleased to be mentioned, leaned her head on me in a gesture of unselfconscious love. The prisoner I am telling you about broke down: 'I wish I could be like Claire, I wish I didn't have to maintain this macho image, I wish someone would put their arms around me.' I was on my feet in seconds, and wrapped my arms round him. It was an unforgettable moment.

One of the other prisoners could not cope with this display of affection. He had no experience of it. He was 26.

We visited 'our lifer' in 'open conditions' prior to his release. I remember driving 630 miles in one day to visit him! He married a lovely Christian girl he had met through reading a church newsletter she had contributed to. At his wedding he gave his buttonhole to our daughter Claire, because she was so special to him. Sadly he died at the age of 46. The irreparable damage done to his body through drug abuse made it impossible for him to withstand leukaemia.

There are people who are sceptical about prison 'conversions'. This one was real!

Not all of us will have such a dramatic turnaround. But there can be few people who do not need delivering from something: bitterness, jealousy, prejudice, envy, over-eating, alcohol abuse, violence, self-indulgence. The list is endless.

So is the healing power of Jesus!

When Jesus crossed the synagogue to heal this woman; when Jesus crossed over from the glory of heaven to live on earth; when he crossed from life to death on Calvary, it was for love of this woman.

For love of me.

For love of you.

Are you stuck at this time in your life, longing to be set free from something that binds you?

The invitation of Jesus remains the same: Come to me.

The OBEDIENT Woman
Matthew 28:1-10

Mary sat by the tomb, wrapped in her grief. As she travelled back through her memories she hugged her arms round herself to stop herself shivering. She glanced at her companion whose eyes were closed. I hope she is sleeping, thought Mary.

She remembered her young life in Magdala. For all that she had money and freedom, she was trapped. Trapped by what others called 'demons'. It was hard to put a name to her suffering. She was shunned and lonely because of her behaviour. She didn't blame those who avoided her, she knew she was strange and bizarre. But she couldn't help herself. She longed to be 'normal'.

She remembered when she had met Jesus, just over a year ago. She had no idea how important he would become in her life. He was staying in the area, and crowds followed him, bringing their sick and suffering. Having no one, Mary had presented herself to Jesus and he had driven out the 'demons' that ruined her life.

For the first time, she was glad she had no husband or protector. When Jesus made it clear she was welcome to join his group of friends, there was no hesitation. She left everything and followed him.

It had been hard at first. She felt she was continually proving herself. It was some time before the rest of the group were able to accept that she really had changed, that this new life and all the means at her disposal were for Jesus and his ministry.

She realised how fortunate she was to be free to follow Jesus, and she knew that her newfound stability came from the role that Jesus had given her.

This year was the year of peace and love.

The year of joy.

The year of God's favour!

She unwrapped every memory, treasuring and savouring every moment she had spent with Jesus.

Brutal reality flooded her mind as she remembered where she was. A few more minutes, she thought, as she waited for the morning star that told her the Sabbath was over. At last she could do what she came to do.

Excruciatingly painful was the memory of the cross. How strange that she, who had been the unstable one, was there right to the end. When even his dearest friends fled, Mary kept watch.

The earth trembled and shook. The women hugged each other in fear, staggering to the tomb.

The stone was moved!

The body was gone!

Terror struck their hearts.

Dazzled by the man in front of them, they heard him say: 'He is not here, he is risen, just as he said. Come and see the place where he lay. Then go quickly and tell his disciples: "He has risen from the dead and is going ahead of you into Galilee. There you will see him." Now I have told you.'

Filled with joy, and yet filled with fear, they ran to tell his disciples.

Suddenly Jesus was there! Mary fell at his feet, clinging on to him.

'Don't be afraid. Go and tell my brothers to go to Galilee, there they will see me.'

As tears shook her body, Jesus held her in his arms. When the torrent of emotion had passed, she remembered Jesus had said, 'Go.'

Go? Where would she go? Jesus was everything! The hardest thing she had ever had to do was to tear herself away from the risen Jesus.

'Tell my brothers,' he had said.

There was the purpose. There was the challenge to fill the void. This was the reason for living: to tell others that Jesus was alive.

She knew she would obey.

How wonderful that Jesus had entrusted himself and the news of his resurrection to Mary. It would have been even more wonderful to say that the men believed her! For the three years they had shared in his ministry, they had seen Jesus treat women with dignity and honour. Yet when it came to it, they had reverted to the conditioning of their past. Jewish men did not accept the witness of a woman! They did not believe her.

They finally found out for themselves that Jesus was indeed alive.

By the time the Holy Spirit fell on both women and men at Pentecost it seems that the problem was resolved.

Or was it?

A few minutes before I went into the pulpit of a large London church, one of the deacons said to me, 'I have to tell you, I don't approve of women preachers!'

Great timing! Just as well I knew that God approves!

John Wesley heard there was a woman preacher in Long Stratton, one of the churches in our area. Having travelled all the way to Norfolk to hear her, he said, 'I own that God is using women in the salvation of souls, and who am I to stand in the way of God?'

Sarah Mallett became one of the first Methodist women local preachers; John Wesley affirmed her role and she did a great work for God in the South Norfolk countryside.

Jesus has provided a role for you in his Church too.

A role uniquely yours.

Have confidence!

Whatever Jesus has called you to do, do it with all your might. Do it for him.

The SEARCHING Woman
John 4:1-30, 39-42

She was always looking for Mr Right.

She laughed a humourless laugh. You would think, after all this time, that she would have given up! The sun pounded down on her head. Noonday, what a time to come to fetch water! The other women from the village had long gone home to their families. Forced to come to the well when no one was about was the price she paid for her lifestyle!

In no way conventional, good-looking and attractive, the woman sighed as she approached the well. 'Soiled' by the men in her life, she thought about the current man. He was as useless as all the others!

Surely there must be a society, somewhere, where a woman could go it alone, where she would not have to depend on a man for protection and provision. Just as well she still had her looks. Surely somewhere, somehow, it was possible to live a clean life, to take her place with the women in the community, to be valued.

Were it not for her faith she would have given up, years ago. At least she was free to worship God on Mount Gerazim, and to fetch her water from the well that Jacob gave to his son Joseph. And she could look forward to the Promised Messiah, God's appointed one who would answer all her questions. Nobody could take that away from her!

Lost in her thoughts, she didn't see a man sitting at the well, until he spoke.

'Will you give me a drink?' the tired stranger asked. He was obviously a Jew and she was a Samaritan. Didn't he know they never mixed?

'How can you ask me for a drink?'

So began the best conversation she had ever had.

In the blazing sun, beside an ancient well, the world-weary woman and the life-giving Jesus discussed theology.

Back and forth the conversation went, over history, need, and spiritual matters. They covered the lot!

Not only did he know how thirsty she was for the living water, he also knew everything else about her. When he made it clear he knew about her lifestyle and the broken relationships, she tried to steer the conversation back to religious matters. Where to worship, for instance: much safer ground! Not so! Jesus spoke of true worshippers worshipping a spiritual God, in spirit. This was all getting too much. She was losing her grip on the discussion. She didn't know if the Jews had got it right, or the Samaritans. 'I know that the Messiah called Christ is coming. When he comes, he will explain everything to us.'

His reply took her breath away. 'I who speak to you am he.'

She knew with total certainty that this was true.

She didn't wait to see the disapproval in Jesus' friends' eyes. She knew all about that!

Thirst forgotten, she left her water pot, hurrying back to the town, to share this amazing news. 'Come and see a man, who told me everything I did. Can this be the Messiah?'

It's a great story. The people hurried to the well, and Jesus talked to them. At their request he went back with them and stayed for two days, long enough for many of the people of the town to become believers. Firstly, they believed because of the woman's testimony. Then they believed because they heard him for themselves. They made a personal choice, based on their own experience of Jesus.

It was when I saw the humanity of Jesus in this story that I first started to love him.

Jesus initiated this conversation.

He crossed barriers of race, culture, class and gender.

Jesus told this woman, who was not accepted in 'polite' society, that he was the Messiah.

Jesus gave this woman his undivided attention.

Jesus gave this woman a mission.

The surprising thing about this story is not that Jesus would treat this woman so, but that his disciples still didn't get the picture! After being with him for so long, you would not think anything about Jesus would surprise them!

Because of the life, death and resurrection of Jesus we have access to God. We have his undivided attention. Not because we are deserving, not because we are well-educated, not because we have 'arrived' socially, not for any other reason than we have put our faith and confidence in Jesus to 'present' us to his Father. You would think the Church would have got the picture, too, wouldn't you?

In first-century Israel, women were not educated. Their role was clearly defined by tradition and teaching.

Jesus reversed all that!

I am a difficult woman to marginalise! I have been part of a loving partnership for 39 years. I've been given freedom, encouragement and confidence by my husband Roy. I am blessed with men friends who value me.

I realise many women are not so fortunate.

I have met many of them. Is that your situation just now?

If you want to know how God feels about you, look at Jesus and his treatment of women. He welcomes you. He affirms you. He values you. He gives you a mission. He gives you a purpose. He loves you. Just as you are!

Don't let anyone put you down!

The KEPT Woman
All the Gospels!

If you have read this far, you will already know a lot about me. By now you will have sussed that I am in love with Jesus. My husband Roy does not see him as a threat: the opposite in fact!

We have shared our faith for nearly 40 years. The platinum blonde he met in 1962, with the cigarette in one hand and the gin and tonic in the other, is long gone. The fiery temper took longer for the Lord to deal with, but the sparkly jewel hidden deep within the layers is still being revealed as each facet is worked on. By the time I join Jesus in glory, I guess it will be completely revealed!

I have mentioned elsewhere how strange are the influences that shape our lives.

I am a very confident driver, useless at navigating, but a confident driver. I am often amazed that I have ended up where I was headed. I usually take the scenic route! Landmarks to me are not pubs and churches, but a stand of lime trees, an incredible rambling rose on the front of a cottage, a water-meadow or an ancient oak.

Shortly after I passed my driving test in the 60s, I crashed our car on some black ice. It went off a bend, turned over and finished up on its roof. It was a wreck and had to be brought home on a trailer. The next morning I needed a vehicle to pick up a visitor from Norwich station 24 miles away. Roy handed me the keys of his van.

Tell me, how many men do you know who would hand over their van to the woman who had just wiped out their car? Roy did. That's confidence for you.

What a picture that is of God and his love for us. Because Jesus separated himself from God on the cross to die in my place, God's forgiveness is available to me. Every day, all day, for as long as it takes!

I have been a 'kept' woman for many years.

This next piece will not go down well in this post-feminist society. So be warned! I am very passionate about women's rights, as all my friends will tell you, but nevertheless, I love being a kept woman.

On my wedding day in 1963, everyone else in the house had gone to the church. My Dad and I were the last to leave. Being an 'East Ender', he had some words of wisdom for me. 'You gonna be all right, mate?' and 'Cor, you look smashin', to name but two!

The vicar asked, 'Who gives this woman in marriage?' My Dad said it was he, and 'gave' me away to Roy.

When I gave my life to God in 1964, God my Father 'gave' me to Jesus. You will read about it in John 6: 37, 39 and 40. Jesus promises he will never, ever let me go.

My heart turns over when I read John 17:24. Jesus said, 'Father, I want those you have given me to be with me where I am, and to see my glory, the glory you have given me because you loved me before the creation of the world.' He wants me, and he wants me to see what he left behind, when he came to earth to die in my place.

Years ago the depression I mentioned elsewhere made me feel trapped. I felt like running away. I would write Roy notes saying I was going to leave him. I was so unhappy. Roy took hours, even days off work to be with me. He would put his hands on my shoulders, look deep into my tear-stained face and say, 'Wherever you go, I will come and find you, and bring you home.' That's what I wanted to hear.

I never left.

I realise I have been incredibly fortunate to have known such earthly love. How blessed, then, to know, that that is how Jesus feels about me. And if that's how he feels about me, that's how he feels about you. Don't just take my word for it, read it for yourself.

Perhaps you have been afraid to take that step, to trust Jesus and give your life to him. There is a lot to lose, for sure. Insecurity and fear, for instance!

There is everything to gain. Purpose, direction, his keeping power and constant presence. His forgiveness, love and peace. His Holy Spirit to make himself real in our lives and to reproduce his character in us. Instant membership into his Family, and, above all, everlasting life.

When I was recovering from a heart attack in 1992, many of my well-meaning friends said, 'Look after yourself, Irene, don't overdo it.'

Impossible! If I had two lives I would give them both to Jesus.

I love him because he first loved me.

And MANY MORE Women . . .

The stories in this book are about women whose lives were changed by their encounters with Jesus, and who lived out a new relationship with him by faith, a relationship and a faith which went far beyond Jesus' death and resurrection, and far beyond anything they could imagine.

And many more women today are living that same life of faith as Jesus Women, in faith trying to change relationships, to challenge injustice, to create a better world for the generations to come.

You are one of the many more women who are following after them – and only you can tell your story.

Are you a Jesus woman?

Traidcraft and Fair Trade

What is Fair Trade, and why is it important?
Fighting poverty through trade

A simple statement, it leads into the complex organisation that Traidcraft is today. It means . . .

- paying people in the 'third world' fair prices
- giving them credit when they need it
- working together for a better future

Millions of people in developing countries don't get a fair share of the wealth created by their own skill and effort and the resources of their land. This is largely because of the way international trade is controlled by the rich countries. It's a system which is both unjust and a major cause of continuing world poverty.

Traidcraft is working to change this injustice by creating opportunities – for the poor in the 'third world' to work their way to a better quality of life, and for people here to join a movement for change that's working for the fairer conduct of international trade.

For more information, please contact:

Traidcraft
Kingsway
Gateshead
Tyne & Wear
NE11 0NE

Tel: 0191 491 0591
Web site: www.traidcraft.co.uk

© Traidcraft, www.traidcraft.co.uk

Acknowledgements

I would like to acknowledge the help of:

My husband Roy, for his constant support.

Claire and Lisa, for allowing me to tell their stories.

Alex Garrard, for sharing his knowledge of the life and times of Jesus.

Bible quotations:

New Revised Standard Version of the Bible, Anglicized Edition copyright 1989, 1995 by the division of Christian Education of the National Council of the Churches of Christ in the USA.

The New International Version Rainbow Study Bible, Rainbow Studies International, El Reno, Oklahoma 73036, USA.